KANSAS

Anita Yasuda

www.av2books.com

Go to **www.av2books.com**, and enter this book's unique code.

BOOK CODE

J549033

AV² by Weigl brings you media enhanced books that support active learning.

AV² provides enriched content that supplements and complements this book. Weigl's AV² books strive to create inspired learning and engage young minds in a total learning experience.

Your AV² Media Enhanced books come alive with...

Audio
Listen to sections of the book read aloud.

Video
Watch informative video clips.

Embedded Weblinks
Gain additional information for research.

Key Words
Study vocabulary, and complete a matching word activity.

Quizzes
Test your knowledge.

Slide Show
View images and captions, and prepare a presentation.

Try This!
Complete activities and hands-on experiments.

... and much, much more!

Published by AV² by Weigl
350 5th Avenue, 59th Floor
New York, NY 10118
Website: www.av2books.com   www.weigl.com

Library of Congress Cataloging-in-Publication Data
Yasuda, Anita.
 Kansas / Anita Yasuda.
   p. cm. -- (Explore the U.S.A.)
 Includes bibliographical references and index.
 ISBN 978-1-61913-351-8 (hard cover : alk. paper)
 1. Kansas--Juvenile literature. I. Title.
 F681.3.Y37 2012
 978.1--dc23
                        2012015074

Printed in the United States of America in North Mankato, Minnesota
1 2 3 4 5 6 7 8 9   16 15 14 13 12

052012
WEP040512

Project Coordinator: Karen Durrie
Art Director: Terry Paulhus

Weigl acknowledges Getty Images as the primary image supplier for this title.

KANSAS

Contents

This is Kansas.
It is called the Sunflower State.
Sunflowers grow in Kansas.

This is the shape of Kansas. Kansas is in the middle part of the United States.

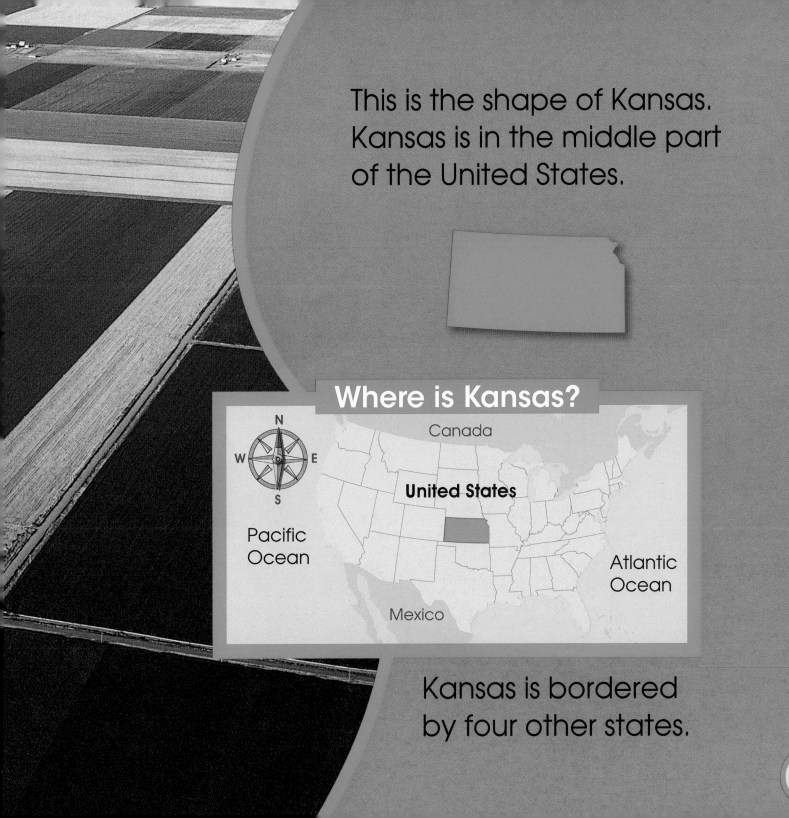

Where is Kansas?

Canada

N
W   E
S

United States

Pacific
Ocean

Atlantic
Ocean

Mexico

Kansas is bordered by four other states.

Amelia Earhart was born in Kansas. She was the first woman to fly across the Atlantic Ocean.

Amelia Earhart disappeared as she tried to fly around the world.

The sunflower is the state flower of Kansas. Sunflowers can turn toward the Sun. Millions of sunflowers grow each year in Kansas.

The Kansas state seal has horses, wagons, and a cabin.

The state seal also has two American Indians hunting bison.

This is the state flag of Kansas. It has the state seal, a sunflower, and the state name.

There is a blue and gold bar under the sunflower.

The Kansas state animal is the American bison. This animal can weigh more than 2,000 pounds. It can run up to 35 miles an hour.

Millions of American bison once roamed the plains of North America.

This is one of the biggest cities in Kansas. It is named Topeka. It is the capital city of Kansas.

The state capitol building in Topeka is one of the largest state capitols.

Security Ber

17

Wheat grows in Kansas. Wheat is used to make flour. Kansas has about 9 million acres of wheat crops.

One stalk of wheat has about 50 seeds.

Kansas is known for its Old West towns.

People visit towns such as Dodge City to learn about how cowboys lived in the past.

KANSAS FACTS

These pages provide detailed information that expands on the interesting facts found in the book. These pages are intended to be used by adults as a learning support to help young readers round out their knowledge of each state in the *Explore the U.S.A.* series.

Pages 4–5

Kansas is the 15th largest state in the United States. The state is known for its rolling fields of wheat and sunflowers. Kansas was named for the Kansa American Indians who lived in the area. On January 29, 1861, Kansas joined the United States as the 34th state.

Pages 6–7

Kansas is bordered by Oklahoma to the south, Colorado to the west, Nebraska to the north, and Missouri to the east. Kansas is also known as America's Heartland because it lies halfway between the East and West coasts of the United States. A large network of roads and railroads serve Kansas. Kansas has the fourth-largest public road system in the United States.

Pages 8–9

Kansas has played an important role in aviation history. The pioneering aviator Amelia Earhart was born in Atchison, Kansas, in 1897. Other important Kansas aviators include William Purvis, Charles Wilson, and Clyde Cessna. Today, there are several major aircraft manufacturers in Wichita, Kansas. Wichita is the world's leading producer of general aviation aircraft.

Pages 10–11

Millions of sunflowers bloom in Kansas each year. The Kansas state seal shows a pioneer scene. There are a wagon train, a farmer plowing a field, and two American Indians on horseback chasing bison. Kansas was opened to settlement in 1854. The 34 stars on the seal represent Kansas as the 34th state.

The Kansas State flag became official in 1927. The flag shows the state seal on a blue background. A sunflower rests on a gold and blue bar above the seal. The bar represents the Louisiana Purchase, a treaty between France and the United States that saw the U.S. double in size. The Louisiana Purchase involved 14 states including Kansas.

At one time, there were up to 70 million American bison in North America. Their population was depleted by about 50 million in the 19th century when settlers hunted the animals for food and sport. Today, there are about 200,000 bison living on preserves and ranches, and about 15,000 wild bison in North America.

In the 1840s, Topeka was an important stop for wagon trains traveling west. Topeka was made the state capital of Kansas by popular vote in 1861. The population of Topeka is about 124,000. The name *Topeka* comes from the Kansa and Iowa American Indian languages. It means "to dig good potatoes."

Kansas is also known as the "Bread Basket of the World." Kansas is a leading state in the production, storage, and export of wheat. The state produces about 370 million bushels of wheat a year. One bushel can make about 45 boxes of wheat cereal. Other important crops grown in Kansas include hay, corn, and alfalfa.

Several sites in Kansas, such as the Santa Fe Trail, offer visitors a glimpse into its early pioneer history. Visitors can still see the ruts made by pioneer wagons more than 100 years ago. Dodge City was founded in 1872. It was a major shipping point for American bison and cattle. It had a reputation as a wild frontier town. Visitors can tour many historic buildings and landmarks.

KEY WORDS

Research has shown that as much as 65 percent of all written material published in English is made up of 300 words. These 300 words cannot be taught using pictures or learned by sounding them out. They must be recognized by sight. This book contains 54 common sight words to help young readers improve their reading fluency and comprehension. This book also teaches young readers several important content words, such as proper nouns. These words are paired with pictures to aid in learning and improve understanding.

Page	Sight Words First Appearance
4	grow, in, is, it, state, the, this
7	by, four, of, other, part, where
8	around, as, first, she, to, was, world
11	a, also, American, can, each, has, Indians, two, year
12	and, name, there, under
15	an, animal, miles, more, once, run, than, up
16	city, one
19	about, used, make
20	for, how, its, learn, lived, old, people, such

Page	Content Words First Appearance
4	Kansas, sunflower
7	shape, United States
8	Amelia Earhart, Atlantic Ocean, woman
11	bison, cabin, flower, horses, millions, seal, Sun, sunflower, wagons
12	bar, flag
15	hour, North America, plains, pounds
16	building, capitol, Topeka
19	acres, crops, flour, seeds, stalk, wheat
20	cowboys, Dodge City, past, towns

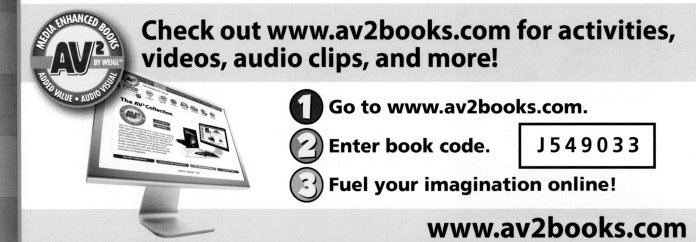